OCEAN DIVERS

Anita Ganeri

Raintree

www.raintreepublishers.co.uk
Visit our website to find out more information about Raintree books.

To order:
☎ Phone 0845 6044371
🖷 Fax +44 (0) 1865 312263
🖳 Email myorders@raintreepublishers.co.uk

Customers from outside the UK please telephone +44 1865 312262

Raintree is an imprint of Capstone Global Library Limited, a company incorporated in England and Wales having its registered office at 7 Pilgrim Street, London, EC4V 6LB – Registered company number: 6695582

Edited by Rebecca Rissman, Dan Nunn, and Sian Smith
Designed by Joanna Hinton Malivoire
Picture research by Elizabeth Alexander
Production by Victoria Fitzgerald
Originated by Capstone Global Library
Printed and bound in China by CTPS

ISBN 978 1 406 22569 3
15 14 13 12 11
10 9 8 7 6 5 4 3 2 1

British Library Cataloguing in Publication Data
Ganeri, Anita, 1961- Ocean divers. -- (Landform adventurers) 1. Oceanographers--Juvenile literature. 2. Oceanography-- Juvenile literature. 3. Ocean--Juvenile literature. I. Title II. Series
551.4'6-dc22

Acknowledgements
We would like to thank the following for permission to reproduce photographs: Corbis pp. 5 (© Michele Westmorland/Science Faction), 9 (© Gary Bell), 13 (© NASA), 14 (© Jeffrey L. Rotman), 20 (© Norbert Wu/ Science Faction), 22 (© Jeffrey L. Rotman), 24 (© Ralph White), 25 (© Julian Calverley), 26 (© Julie Dermansky); Getty Images pp. 10 (Steve Mason/Photodisc), 18 (Ira Block/National Geographic); © Image Quest Marine p. 17; Photo by Advanced Imaging & Visulization Lab p. 21 (©Woods Hole Oceanographic Institution); Photolibrary pp. 7 (Purestock), 11 (imagebroker), 27 (Enrico Sacchetti); Science Photo Library pp. 6 (Alexis Rosenfeld), 12 (Martin Jakobsson), 15 (Klein Associates), 16 (Georgette Douwma), 19 (Alexis Rosenfeld), 28 (Simon Fraser), 29 (Matthew Oldfield); Shutterstock pp. 4 (© Map Resources), 8 (© Specta), 23 (© Brandelet).

Cover photograph of Caribbean reef sharks reproduced with permission of Photolibrary (David B Fleetham/OSF).

Some words are shown in bold, like this. You can find out what they mean by looking in the glossary.

Contents

What are oceans?

Oceans are huge stretches of salty water. They cover about two-thirds of the Earth. There are five oceans: the Pacific, Atlantic, Indian, Southern, and Arctic.

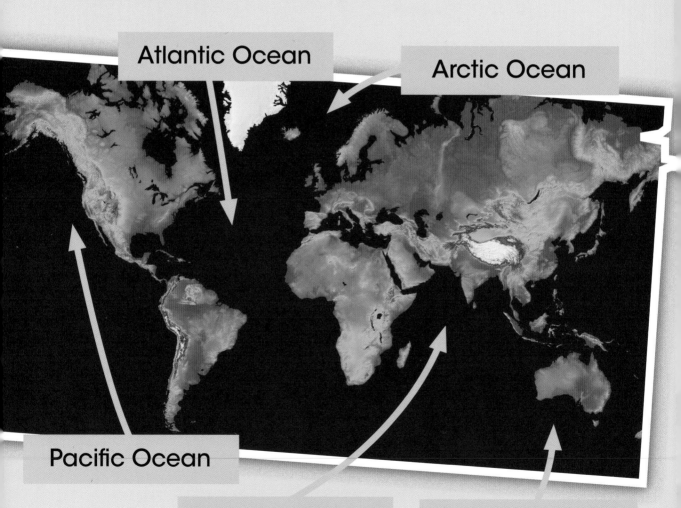

Atlantic Ocean

Arctic Ocean

Pacific Ocean

Indian Ocean

Southern Ocean

From colourful coral reefs to the dark, deep sea, oceans are brilliant places for scientists to explore. Are you ready to dive in?

Exploring the oceans

Scientists who study the oceans are called **oceanographers**. They look at sea plants and animals, underwater geography, such as volcanoes, and sunken shipwrecks.

Oceanographers have lots of ways of studying the oceans. They use ships with special **instruments**, computers, **submersibles**, and even **satellites** in outer space.

OCEAN FACT
Satellites look at waves, sea temperature, and ocean **pollution**.

Remarkable reefs

Where can you see fish that look like butterflies, starfish, and giant clams? The answer is on a coral reef. The Great Barrier Reef in Australia is so big that it can be seen from space!

Huge coral reefs grow in warm oceans.

OCEAN FACT
Coral reefs are built by tiny animals, called **coral polyps.**

Ocean diving

Marine biologists dive underwater to look at life on a coral reef. They have to wear special **scuba diving** suits. They carry tanks of air on their backs to breathe. They may also carry underwater cameras to take photos of the creatures they see.

fin

OCEAN FACT
Divers wear flipper-like fins on their feet to help them swim.

Seabed features

You might think the seabed is flat. But it has mountains, valleys, and volcanoes, just like the land! The Mid-Atlantic Ridge is a chain of mountains in the Atlantic Ocean. It is more than 16,000 kilometres long. That's over 14 times the length of Great Britain!

Mid-Atlantic ridge

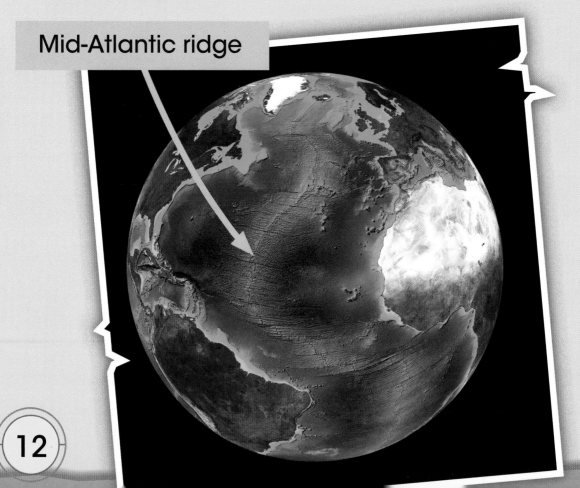

OCEAN FACT
The islands of Hawaii are the tops of underwater volcanoes.

Using sound

Scientists have special **instruments** that use sound to make maps of the seabed, showing what it looks like. They are called **sonar** instruments. Ships on the surface pull the instruments across the seabed.

OCEAN FACT
Sonar can even be used to find underwater shipwrecks!

shipwreck

Atlantic Ocean, Buzzards Bay, USA

15

Fiery fountains

In 1977 scientists saw fountains of hot water gushing up from **vents** in the seabed. They also found giant tube worms and other extraordinary animals living around the vents.

vent

OCEAN FACT
Giant tube worms can grow to more than three metres long. That's taller than a person!

Mini submarines

Scientists travel in mini submarines called **submersibles** to explore the deep sea. It is cramped and cold inside a submersible. But it is exciting to look out the windows as it sinks deeper and deeper.

submersible

OCEAN FACT
It can take a submersible about three hours to dive 4,000 metres.

Roving robots

A **trench** is a deep dip in the ocean floor. It can be dangerous for scientists to dive into trenches. Instead, they send robots called ROVs (Remote-Operated Vehicles). Scientists on board a ship work the ROVs. The ROVs have lights and cameras for taking pictures.

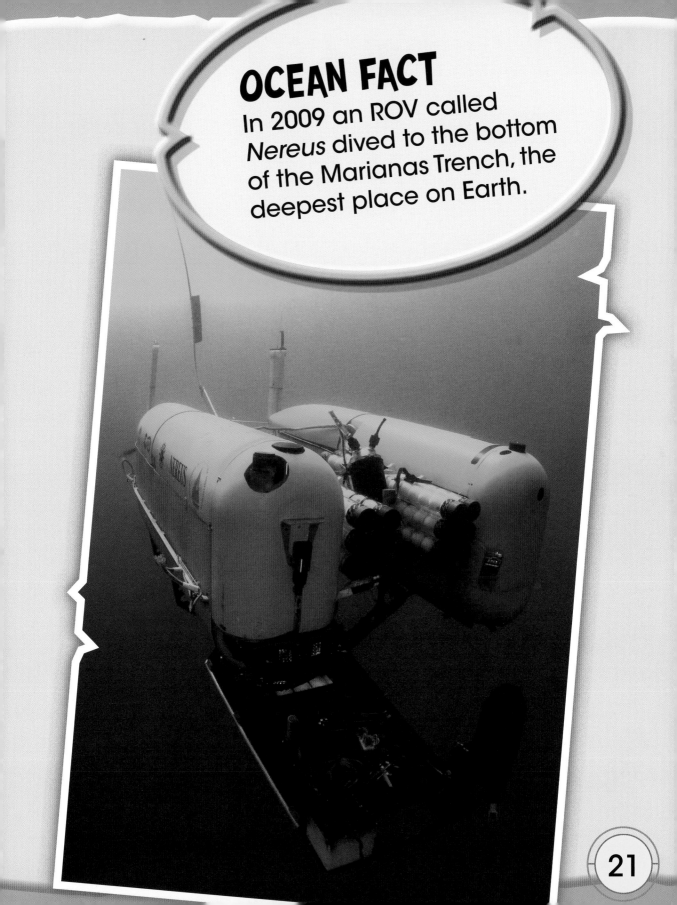

OCEAN FACT
In 2009 an ROV called *Nereus* dived to the bottom of the Marianas Trench, the deepest place on Earth.

Studying wildlife

Scientists who study ocean wildlife are called **marine biologists**. One of their jobs is to tag sharks. First, they track the shark by boat. Then they fix a tag to its back fin. By following the tagged sharks, scientists can learn more about where they swim.

shark

whale shark

OCEAN FACT

The biggest fish in the sea is the whale shark. It can grow 18 metres long. That's almost the same length as two double-decker buses!

Shipwreck!

In 1985 an ROV called *Argo* found the wreck of the *Titanic*. The *Titanic* was a famous ship that sank in 1912 when it hit an iceberg.

Argo

OCEAN FACT

Marine archaeologists look for shipwrecks and sunken cities under the sea. Sometimes, they even find long-lost pirate treasure.

Oil spill

In April 2010 an oil rig exploded in the Gulf of Mexico. Huge amounts of oil spilled into the sea. This led to **pollution** on the shore and it killed wildlife. Scientists used planes and **satellites** to check how the oil spread. Ships sucked up some of the oil.

ROV controls

OCEAN FACT
ROVs were sent down into the sea to try to stop the pipe leaking.

Becoming an oceanographer

If you want to be an **oceanographer**, you need to be good at science. You may also need to study a subject such as **marine biology** at university.

Being an oceanographer is an exciting career. You might be based in a laboratory on land for some of the time. But you may also get to travel to oceans all over the world!

Glossary

coral polyps tiny sea creatures, related to jellyfish, that build coral reefs

instruments equipment used by scientists

marine archaeologist scientist who studies ancient ruins and objects found in the sea

marine biologist scientist who studies living things in the sea

marine biology study of living things in the sea

oceanographer scientist who studies oceans

pollution making the sea dirty by dumping chemicals, rubbish, or oil into it

satellites devices in space that travel round the Earth and collect information

scuba diving diving in a wetsuit with an aqualung (tank of air) on the back

sonar instrument that uses sound to make maps of the seabed

submersible vehicle like a mini submarine, used for exploring the deep sea

trench deep valley under the sea

vent opening in the Earth's crust from which gases escape

Find out more

Find out

Where is the deepest point in the ocean?

Books

100 Things You Should Know about Extreme Earth, Belinda Gallagher
(Miles Kelly, 2009)

Horrible Geography: Odious Oceans, Anita Ganeri
(Scholastic Children's Books, 2008)

My World of Geography: Oceans, Vicky Parker
(Heinemann Library, 2005)

Oceans Atlas with CD-ROM, John Woodward
(Dorling Kindersley, 2007)

Websites

news.bbc.co.uk/cbbcnews/hi/ newsid_6930000/newsid_6935100/6935143.stm
Play a game to explore the deep sea and discover some extraordinary creatures.

oceanservice.noaa.gov/kids
Find out lots of information and amazing facts from the NOAA kids' site.

Index